Tree Houses

ROYAL BARRY WILLS

with illustrations by the author and Charles H. Crombie

1 9 5 7

HOUGHTON MIFFLIN COMPANY BOSTON

The Riverside Press Cambridge

ACKNOWLEDGMENTS

The author wishes to express his appreciation to

Charles H. Crombie, who was of infinite help with the sketches

Leon Keach, for his help with the diagrams and directions

Vilmar K. Bose, for his able editing of the text

Virginia Bohlin, for her helpful criticism

Thanks are also due to my Associates

MERTON S. BARROWS and ROBERT E. MINOT

CONTENTS

This book is dedicated to my nephew, Bob Harris,

who with his friends built the original tree house

that grew down to the ground.

THE HOUSE THAT GREW DOWN FROM A TREE

I'VE SEEN a lot of tree houses but I've only seen one like the house my nephew Bob and his friend Ricky built. Their house intrigued me so much that I decided to write this book. It all began the summer Ricky was eleven and Bob ten. For years they had spent more time up in the trees all around town than they had spent on the ground. They were expert climbers, and more than that, they knew what each tree was especially good for. They would sit high up in the tall birch trees and sway back and forth in the wind. Or they would climb over from one of the tall strong trees to the very top of a small limber birch and swoop down to the ground like flying squirrels.

Their favorite trees were oaks, each one like a fortress, with many strong thick branches growing out on all sides. They were sitting up in one of the giant oaks near Ricky's grandmother's house one day when they got the idea of building themselves a tree house. In its first stage the house was more "strung up" than built: they found some old gunny sacks which they split open and hung from the branches, lacing them together with string.

Then they decided they needed a floor so that they could walk around instead of having to stay on the branches. They collected as much wood as they could find

— driftwood and old lumber lying about unused. Almost any boards would do so long as they were strong. When the boys tried to nail the boards to the tree they had a hard time, because no two branches were exactly the same height and the floor kept coming out crooked. They found some heavy timbers for beams and I showed them how to use a spirit level. At last they got the beams spiked to the tree and the boards nailed across level. They still used the gunny sacks for walls, and since the roof was open they could look up at the sky.

By the next summer they decided they wanted a real house — not something that was half tent and half house.

Again they combed through scrap piles until they found enough wood to build

a new floor. They framed their walls with 2 x 4's, which they nailed to the new floor. Next came the roof, covered with some tar paper salvaged from the scrap pile. The rest of the tar paper was used to cover the boards on the sides of their house. Old cellar windows that could be opened and closed were appropriated, and a ladder

replaced the old cleats.

The house was complete when they
added a door from the old hen
shed, strengthened with corner braces.

By this time it was August and only a few weeks remained before school re-opened. The boys decided to take advantage of every moment by moving into the tree house at once. This meant that they would need beds so that they could sleep out, too. At first they made their beds out of pine boughs (cut from low branches in order not to injure the pine trees), but when the branches dried out and stuck into them they had to substitute mattresses for the old evergreen branches. The mattresses took up so much space that the boys finally hit on the idea of building bunks. Old 2 x 4's made good frames and posts. The top ends of the posts were fastened to the roof. They doubled the gunny sacks and stretched them across the frames, nailing them underneath. Then the mattresses were put on top.

The next morning they realized that cold breakfast was cold comfort, so they set off for the junk yard in search of a stove. After four days of poking around they found an old pot-bellied wood stove, which they immediately christened "Old Ironsides." They hauled it up into the tree house in sections; then they cut a hole in the wall and ran the stack through the hole and up three feet above the roof.

Now, with stove and all, the boys felt the need of keeping their tree house a private place of their own. They put a padlock on the door and tacked up a "No Trespassing" sign.

But there was one trespasser that paid no heed to their warning: the hurricane! To be sure, before the boys were forced to leave their tree house, they had tied it down as securely as they could in the face of the howling September wind. But the morning after the storm they looked across a wrecked field to the old oak tree. The tree house was still there — that is, what was left of it.

All the leaves and half the branches had blown off the tree. The house slanted precariously. The door was gone, and the ladder, too. The wall was broken, the window glass had blown out, and a corner of the roof had pulled loose.

As they looked about them at the wreckage, they were very sad. They knew they could repair the house, but the tree would never be the same again. It was September and school would be starting soon. There would only be a few short

hours each day for work. The least they could do now was to prop up the house.

It was no problem to find two strong posts, but under the circumstances propping up was not an easy job. However, they found that by laying some boards on the ground and wedging them under the posts, they could hammer them in and under tightly and firmly. Then they drove spikes in through the floor beams to fasten the posts at the top.

Standing back, looking up at the house in the tree with its two legs reaching down to the ground, both boys were struck by one thought. If they had four posts that went right to the ground, and boards were put from one to the other, their tree house could have *a downstairs part!* It would be more like a regular house; but they wouldn't be deserting their oak tree, and instead of a house in the tree, they would have a tree in the house.

That evening they came to my home just bubbling with ideas. By the time they left they were prepared to design their house according to the plans we had worked out together on the big drawing table in my study.

The old tree house would become an upstairs bedroom. Directly under it, at ground level, was to be the new kitchen (and new home of "Old Ironsides"), and behind the kitchen another bedroom. You see in Drawing 2 how the original roof was to be continued down over the bedroom in the manner of an old "salt-box" house. Then to get a living room they would extend the first floor, as shown on my plan, and put a less steep "shed roof" over it and the new bathroom in back (see Drawing 3).

The tree would be entirely *inside* the house and a ladder on the trunk would still make a good stairway to the upstairs bedroom. They would need more windows. When I asked them how they were going to meet expenses, they quickly calculated that by pooling their savings and foraging for scraps and secondhand materials they could come out all right — especially if they could count on me to show them how to get the most for their money.

And they did come out all right by dint of good hard work, even though there were some trying times. They got under way the following summer, replacing the two prop-up posts with four new posts set on solid cement bases, and directly under the corners of the original tree house. When it came to boarding up the first floor, they discovered to their chagrin that they had forgotten to leave a door between the kitchen and the downstairs bedroom. It wasn't easy for them to go by a *plan*. However, they decided to cut the door through later if they wanted it badly enough, and that experience helped them remember to leave a front-door opening on the other side of the kitchen.

On the side toward the new living room they nailed a thick piece of wood from one post to the other, about six inches below the floor of the tree house above. They figured that this would serve as a place to rest the 2 x 4 pieces of lumber for the living-room roof, and they did this carefully, using a spirit level to get it plumb. Then they put up two more large posts on cement bases, about fifteen feet away from the kitchen wall. These were the two far corners of the living room and they carried a solid beam on which the other end of the roof timbers

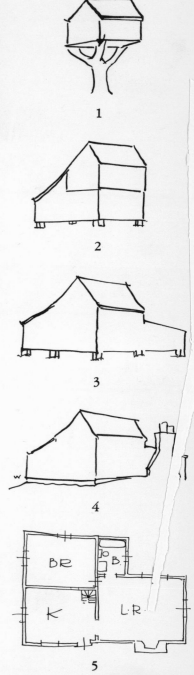

1

2

3

4

5

would rest. When the sides and roof were added the living room took shape.

Next they set the corner posts for the bedroom and the little bathroom and I told them how to extend the tree house roof down over the bedroom. The bath was roofed like the living room, with a "shed" roof. Fixtures for the bathroom were picked up in a junk yard; and that was easy compared to the problems of supplying running water and drainage. They would need pipes, which meant space beneath the floor, which in turn meant a cellar.

While wrestling in their minds with the solution to this problem, they busied themselves repairing damages to the roof and windows, and adding screens to keep out flies and mosquitoes. As Ricky was coming down the ladder one day he gave his head a nasty bump on a branch of the tree, with the result that the old oak had to be sawed down and a winding staircase built. Only the stump remained. This served as a fine table and a lasting memento of the tree.

Already five summers of tree-house living had passed. The sturdy oak was gone — all but the stump. The tree house had grown down to the ground.

Bob and Ricky now had a house with four small rooms — three spreading out below and one upstairs. And a bathroom, of course, but there was still no running water to the bathroom and kitchen.

It was their sixth summer when they started the hardest work of all — digging the cellar under the house. While digging, the boys ran into a spring. At this moment a neighbor passed and advised them to dig a ditch out toward the lower side of the land down to the creek and put a clay pipe in to take off the water.

Finally, after months of back-breaking work, the foundation was completed, the pipes put in and connected to the water main, and a heating unit installed.

Thus it was that a strung-up gunny-sack tree house in an oak tree grew down into a fine substantial house on the ground. It started as a boyish impulse, but a few years after it was completed Bob and Ricky sold the house for a considerable sum of money to a young married couple who lived in it the year round, and they were just as comfortable as could be.

Trees

THERE ARE as many different ways of building tree houses as there are different kinds of
trees. In the following pages I will show you
some of the variations I have seen. Then I
will describe in detail, step by step, how to
build a house in a single tree, and after this
the steps involved in a house built between
two trees.

You may want to follow one of these sets
of plans, or you may not, but it would be a
good idea to study them carefully so that you
have the information in case you need it.
You will probably find that the same general
steps hold true for all tree houses. However,
I think your house will work out better if
you plan ahead, a stage at a time, than if you
build in too much of a hurry.

First of all, you want to find the right tree.
A large tree that branches out broadly not too
high above the ground is apt to be better
than one that has a long straight trunk with

Apple

Beech

many thin branches. The only exception to this is a house built between two trees below the branches (see page 16). Generally speaking, though, you will be better off if your tree has several thick, low branches — strong arms to support your floor — at about the same height above the ground.

Trees like the elm (if not too tall), willow, oak, maple, beech, and apple very often branch out low to make a natural place for a tree house. Sometimes the common pine will do this, but usually it is too straight and tall to be good for building in — unless you decide on a two-tree house.

As you look for your tree you will probably find that you are seeing many things about trees that you never noticed before — their various shapes, what kind of leaf and bark each has, where and how they live. You may want to know more, how hard or soft their wood is, for instance, how brittle or easily split. Look for the books listed below in your school or public library:

The Boy Scout Handbook
First Book of Trees by Maribelle Cormack
Trees and Trails by Clarence John Hylander
Trees: A Guide to Familiar American Trees

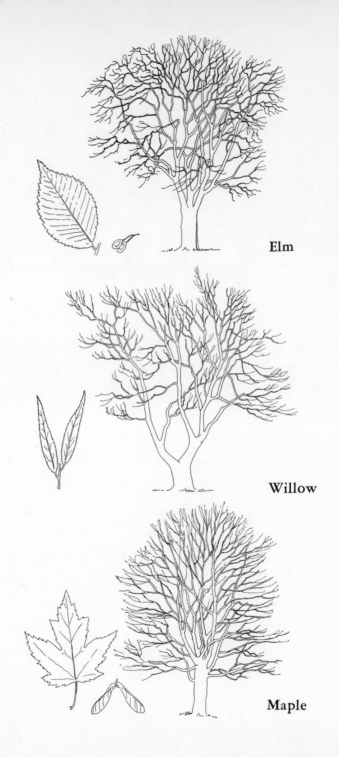

Elm

Willow

Maple

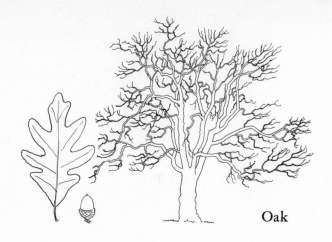

Oak

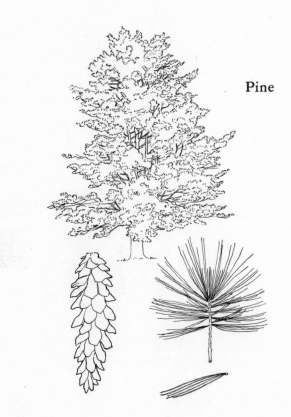

Pine

by Herbert Spencer Zim and Martin Alexander Campbell

Knowing Your Trees by G. H. Collingwood and W. D. Brush

A Natural History of Trees of Eastern and Central North America by Donald Culross Peattie

A Natural History of Western Trees by Donald Culross Peattie.

In the drawings that follow you will see a number of different tree houses. Notice the ways they vary, but notice especially the differences in the trees, and how in each case the house has been fitted to the particular formation of the branches. Look carefully at the big timbers under each house to see how they rest on the supporting branches.

A One-tree House

Here is a very simple one I saw once, built like a "lean-to." On one side of the tree two big branches grew off at about the same height. These and the trunk formed a good three-point support for the house. The blanket was hung up in front to shade the floor from the sun, and I suppose it was partly dropped down when the weather was windy or rainy.

A Three-tree House

This next one, which is also simple in construction, was built between three trees. Perhaps the person who built it couldn't find a single tree big enough to support a house in its branches, but did see these three trees growing close together and so decided to build from one to the other.

Notice how the two poles, or logs, under the house were used to make a big V between the trees. The floor was then built on top of the V and the wider part was covered with a roof. The narrower part of the V made a good landing, or porch.

A Four-tree House

These trees — no one of them big enough by itself to support a tree house — all happened to be so evenly spaced that they were almost like the legs on a table. All together they made an ideal place for a tree house.

Boards between two of the closer trees provided a wide ladder up to the house.

A Two-tree House

Here is a two-tree house. Look at the large pieces of wood under the floor. On each tree there is a Y-shaped support with a horizontal piece on top. This is called a "brace." The boys who built this tree house put up the two big braces first, one on each tree, nailed tight at top and bottom. (You will find the steps for building a brace under the instructions for building a two-tree house, on pages 50–51.) Then they put two heavy timbers all the way across from one brace to the other. When this was done, they laid boards across the two timbers to make a floor, and the rest of the house went on top of that.

Another Two-tree House

At first this house looks just like the last one. However, you will see that there is a brace on only *one* tree — the one farther away — instead of on both trees.

The nearer tree made its own natural brace because its branches grew like a Y. All that was needed was a good strong piece across the top of the Y, like the piece on top of the brace made on the opposite tree. Then the timbers across, and so on.

17

Tools

Once you have found your tree, your next step is to gather tools and building materials. You don't need to have all your materials at the start — you can add to them as you go along. But here are some you will need sooner or later.

COMMON TOOLS

Hammer — a full-sized "claw hammer"

Saw — a full-sized saw, about 26″ long, with fairly coarse teeth, called a "crosscut" saw

Screwdriver

Hand drill

Measure — a 6′ steel tape or folding wood rule

Ladder — a common ladder that isn't too large to handle easily, the wider the better (*not* a folding step ladder)

Rope — a thin, twisted hemp rope (*not* braided clothesline, twine, or heavy string)

Pulley

OTHER LESS COMMON TOOLS

There are three tools you may not have used before, but you will find them necessary for making parts straight, level, or square. If you learn to use these tools all through your work, you will find that parts will fit together tighter and that your tree house will look better than if you judged by eye alone.

TRY SQUARE

Try Square. A wood or metal block with a steel edge ruled off in inches.

It is used to make a line square across a board. Be sure that the block is tight against the side of the board and the steel edge flat before you draw the line. Always use a sharp pencil. If this is done carefully, and you keep your crosscut saw on the line, your board will be cut off square.

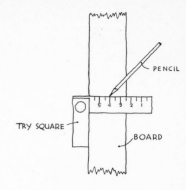

Spirit Level. A smooth piece of wood or metal with a semicircular hole (marked A in drawing) cut in the middle of one edge. In the hole is a horizontal glass tube filled with oily liquid in which there is an air bubble; you will notice when you tilt the level that the bubble moves back and forth in the tube. Two small marks on the tube tell you when the bubble is exactly in the center. A spirit level is used to test whether a horizontal surface or board is level with the ground. Place the level on the surface with the semicircular hole on top; it is level when the bubble is exactly in the center of the tube. Some levels have a second hole (marked B) cut through at one end. This hole is generally round and has a vertical glass tube with an air bubble inside. This will tell you whether a surface is straight up and down vertically.

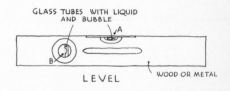

Plumb Line. This is a heavy cotton string at one end of which is attached a metal piece called a plumb bob, usually pointed at the bottom. When the string is let out and the plumb bob hangs freely, the plumb line indicates a straight vertical line. If you are putting up a post, let the plumb line hang down without touching anything. When it stops swinging, look at the post and the string and see if they are parallel. Adjust your post till the edge of it looks as straight up and down as the plumb line.

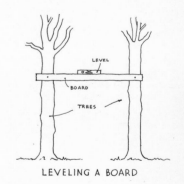

LEVELING A BOARD

Wood and Other Materials

You will need quite a lot of wood to build your tree house — in fact, a good deal more than you think! A pile of wood may look big, but when you start cutting it to proper sizes (wasting a certain amount), and fitting it all together, you will probably find it doesn't go far enough. Fortunately, you don't need much *new* wood. New wood from the lumber yard is quite expensive. If you keep your eyes open for discarded wood, you will be able to gather enough for most of your needs. It may be necessary to clean up this used wood. Pull out the nails and cut away the parts that are rotten, cracked, or too uneven. Most tree houses are built of such used lumber. Use only wood that is at least $3/4''$ thick. The thin wood from apple boxes is not strong enough for most purposes.

Carpenters have a convenient system for identifying lumber by its size. A piece of lumber that is $2''$ thick and $4''$ wide is called a two-by-four (2 x 4); a board $1''$ thick and $8''$ wide is called a one-by-eight (1 x 8). The thickness of the wood is the first dimension given, and the width of the piece the second. These common wood sizes are based on the measurements of the lumber when it was cut at the sawmill. Before you buy it from the lumber yard it goes through one more operation — it is planed down smooth on all four sides. As a result, it is no longer quite $2''$ thick or quite $4''$ wide, but probably measures $1 5/8'' \times 3 5/8''$. In spite of the fact that it is slightly thinner and narrower, it is still called by its full size, $2'' \times 4''$.

These are the common wood sizes which will be most helpful to you in building a tree house. When planed, all of these are about $3/4''$ thick:

1 x 3	1 x 8
1 x 4	1 x 10
1 x 6	1 x 12

These are about $1\frac{5}{8}''$ thick when planed:

2 x 4	2 x 6

Sometimes you will find it useful to use wider or thicker pieces of wood, but not often. Thicker pieces are good for posts and beams and other parts of a house "frame" — the skeleton of the house onto which the boards are nailed. You are probably familiar with "plywood." This comes in large, flat pieces, and is made mechanically by cutting thin layers of wood and gluing them together under pressure to the proper thickness. Very often one large sheet of waterproof plywood is used in place of a lot of narrow boards. It can be used, if you happen to have some on hand, for a floor (on top of heavy pieces which frame the floor), or for the outside of a wall or for roof covering. But do not use plywood alone without thick pieces of wood to support it. It bends easily. A plywood floor, for example, would probably fall through unless there were heavy timbers under it to give it strength.

NAILS

You will need a large quantity of nails. Used nails are not as good as used wood because once nails are bent it is almost impossible to straighten them out. Nails are sold by the pound or by the keg. You will probably find it best to buy only about five pounds or less each time. The size of nails, unlike wood, is not given in inches, but in what is called "pennies." This is a measurement that goes back to the old days when nails were sold by the hundred, and the number of pennies charged per hundred indicated the size of the nail, small nails costing less than large ones. Here are some common sizes of nails and their equivalent lengths in inches.

COMMON WIRE NAILS

Size	Length
Sixpenny nail	2" long
Eightpenny nail	2½" long
Tenpenny nail	3" long
Twentypenny nail	4" long
Fortypenny nail	5" long
Sixtypenny nail	6" long

These sizes are about all you will need. You will want what are called "common" nails — the ones with large, flat heads. If I say you should use a "spike," I simply mean that you should use a large nail (fortypenny or sixtypenny size). If you put tar paper or roofing on your tree house, you will need "roofing nails." These are usually about an inch long, with a very large flat head.

Don't get too many nails at one time. Keep them dry and they won't rust. Learn to hammer them in tight and try to place them wisely so that a few nails will do most of the work.

Building a One-tree House

Tree houses built in one tree are the most common ones. I will describe the steps in building a one-tree house first, and then tell how to build a two-tree house. Since the problems are different and a one-tree house is not always the easiest kind to build, be sure to study both sets of instructions carefully before you start to build either kind of house. You may decide to combine or modify these plans in order to fit your own situation and needs.

Here, generally speaking, are the important steps in building a one-tree house:

1. Placing underpinning timbers in the tree so as to give you a level foundation on which to build the platform.
2. Placing beams on the underpinning, or foundation, to frame a platform with heavy supporting pieces.
3. Laying the floor joists.
4. Laying the floor boards.
5. Framing the walls.
6. Framing the roof.
7. Framing the windows.
8. Enclosing the house by nailing boards onto the wall and roof frames.
9. Finishing the house, roofing, etc.

For a single-tree house like the one shown in the pictures that follow, the ideal tree is one with several strong low branches spreading out at about the same level, and with none of the main branches growing directly up out of the center. Our tree house is a fairly large one. You may want to simplify yours, and it will be up to you to decide what shape and size will best fit your tree.

FIRST STEP: *Placing underpinning timbers*

The very first problem you will have to solve is how to get a level starting place, or "foundation," for your house. Of course, the branches of the tree are uneven, but you don't want your floor uneven. This is why you start by placing some heavy timbers (marked A) on the strongest branches. See Figure 1.

The underpinning timbers (A) should be heavy wood, 4 x 4's or larger, or two 2 x 4's nailed together (to nail two 2 x 4's together, drive sixteenpenny nails into them every 12″).

These timbers need not come together at the ends, but it is most important that they be the same height from the ground, and as level as possible. Test them with your spirit level; you may need to insert wedges or props to make them level. Be sure that the supporting branches are strong and that the distance between the timbers is not too great for the beams to span.

When your underpinning timbers are level, but before you nail them down, you will be ready for the second step.

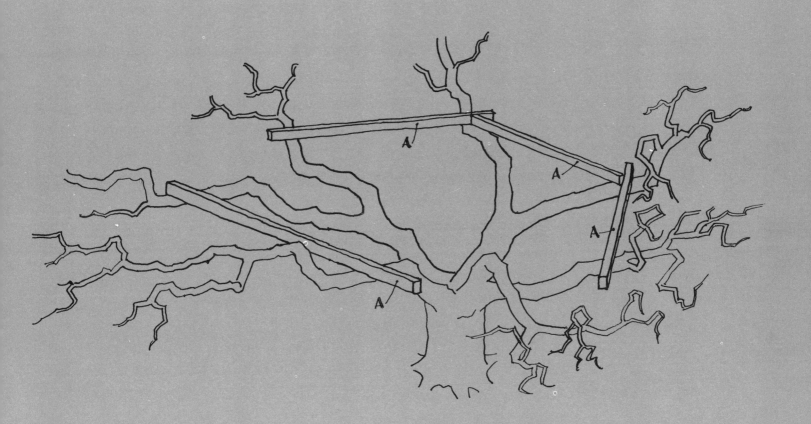

Figure 1

SECOND STEP: *Placing beams on the foundation*

Figure 2 shows the beams (marked B) laid across the underpinning. The beams should be as heavy as the underpinning timbers; they should be placed parallel to each other and about 4' apart. Two of them should be about 2' longer than the other in order to support a small landing later. Be sure that each beam is level. Also, lay a board flat across them and put your spirit level on the board to find out if the beams are level with each other. You may have to move your underpinning timbers a little one way or another until the beams are supported level. Now nail the underpinning timbers to the branches using large nails, forty-penny or fiftypenny size.

Timbers and beams all level, you are now ready to nail the beams to the underpinning timbers. Drive twentypenny nails at a slant near the bottom edges of the beams deep down into the foundation timbers. This is called "toenailing" and is a method you will often use. In this way spike all the beams to the timbers from both sides wherever they cross.

This is perhaps the hardest step in tree-house building — getting off to a level start. Take your time to get this done properly. Make your foundation firm, securely nailed and supported by the tree at as many places as possible.

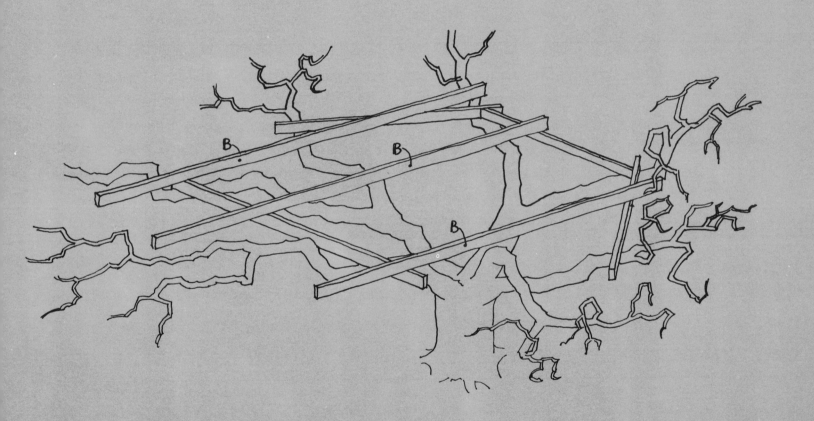

Figure 2

THIRD STEP: *Laying floor joists*

In Figure 3 you see the C pieces laid across and at right angles to the beams; these are called floor joists. Later your floor boards will be laid directly on them.

The floor joists should be 2 x 4's or 2 x 6's and they should be cut long enough so that they stick out 4″ at each end beyond the beams. Placed upright on edge, the floor joists won't bend as easily as they would if they were laid on the flat side. It is these joists that are supposed to keep your floor from bending or sagging.

All the joists run in the same direction, that is, across the beams. They should be no more than 2′ apart, all spaced the same distance from each other.

Keep the joist at each end of your foundation about 3″ in from the tips of the beams.

Once the joists are in place, toenail them onto the beams at each point where they cross.

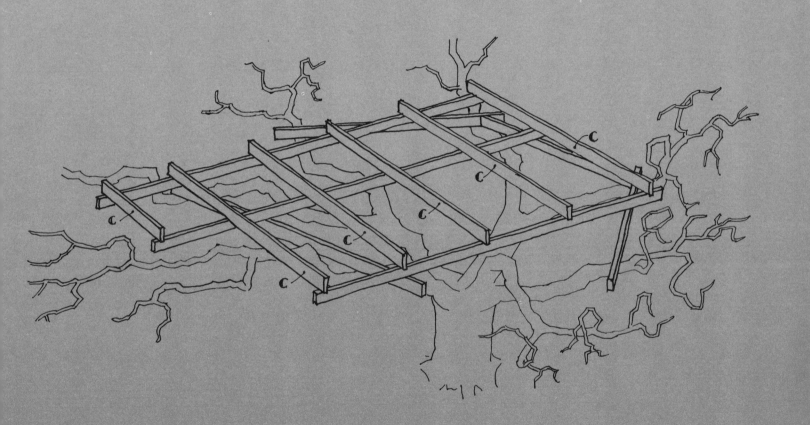

Figure 3

FOURTH STEP: *Laying the floor boards*

Floor boards may be of inch-thick wood (it is actually about ¾″ thick) and of varying widths. They are laid crosswise on the C pieces, or joists. Let the ends of the joists stick out 4″ beyond the floor boards on each side. This is very important. When you come to nailing the upright supports for the walls you will see why.

Some of your boards may be long enough to go all the way across the floor. If not, cut your shorter pieces so that they end at the center of the nearest joist. Start the board that goes the rest of the way across the floor on this same joist. In this way all the ends of shorter boards will be right on joists and fully supported.

In Figure 4 you will see how your floor may look.

Figure 4

FIFTH STEP: *Framing the walls*

In Figure 5 you will understand more clearly why two of the beams were kept 2′ longer than the other; and why the joists were left uncovered 4″ beyond the floor boards on each side. The extra 2′ on the beams is for a small landing for the ladder; and you will nail all the upright supports for walls and railings to the ends of the joists.

The pieces marked D are 2 x 4's about 3′ long which serve as posts for the railing around your porch. You can use your plumb line to make sure these posts are straight up and down. At the foot of each post, drive three sixteen-penny nails into the joist and three more into the beam below. Then you can nail on the railing boards, some near the top of the posts, and some halfway down to the floor.

Next, cut the E pieces, which are called "studs." They should be about 5′ or 6′ long — at any rate long enough so that when they are nailed up in position the top ends will be above your head. Of course, they should all be sawed exactly the same length.

Nail each of the E pieces carefully to the ends of the joists and to the beams below in the same fashion as you nailed the posts. These nails will later be carrying a lot of weight — most of the weight of the walls and roof of your house. Be sure they are holding tightly.

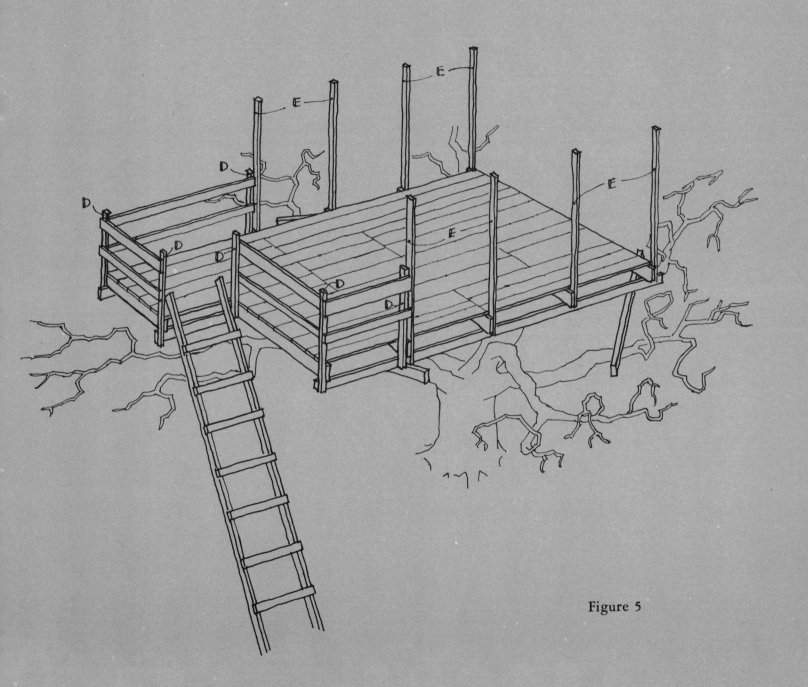

Figure 5

In Figure 6 you see two pieces of wood, marked F, laid across the tops of all the E pieces. These F pieces are called "plates." To find the proper length for F, measure from the outside of the first stud to the outside of the last one, at the bottom. Saw F just this length, and nail it to the top of each stud with two nails.

Now cut two pieces, marked G, just long enough to go from the outside of one wall to the outside of the other. Nail them up inside the first and last studs and underneath the plates F.

If there is any tendency of the frame to sway or move or wobble, nail some boards inside the studs, diagonally for the time being. This will brace them and make them steadier.

U. S. 1000846

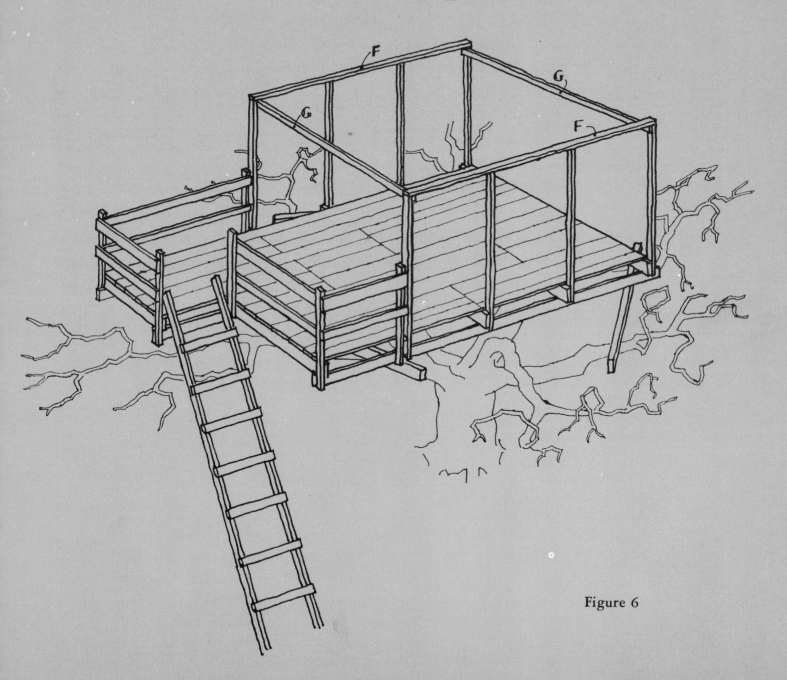

Figure 6

35

A roof that is sloped two ways has a "ridgepole" at the center, marked H in Figure 7. But first we must nail up some wood to support the ridgepole.

Cut two 2 x 4's about 3' longer than the studs of the wall. These are marked I. Measure along G and find the center; from this point measure 1' on each side and stand the I pieces up at these points outside G. Check with your plumb line to be sure that they are vertical and then nail them to G at the top and to the floor at the bottom by slanting nails down through them into the floor boards. Later your door will come between these two I pieces.

The pieces marked J are similar to the I pieces except that they should be 6" longer, because they will be nailed to the joist instead of the floor. Stand them up as you did the I pieces. One person will have to hold the piece in place while the other nails it to the joist at the bottom and to the G piece above. These J pieces will not need to be as close to each other as the I pieces are; it is best to space them the same distance from the corners of the house as from each other.

Now nail the K pieces across between the I pieces at one end and the J pieces at the other. Make sure that they are both level and the same distance above the floor.

Following this, measure the floor and mark the exact center of the floor under the two K pieces. Hold your plumb line on the K pieces so that the plumb bob points to the center marks, and mark the centers of the K pieces.

The ridgepole, marked H, should now be cut. It should be a 1 x 6 or a 2 x 6 board, as long as the distance from the outside edges of both K pieces plus an extra 4" at each end. Place the ridgepole H along the two center marks on the K pieces, standing it on its narrow edge. To hold it up in this position while you are building, you may brace it temporarily with small pieces of wood, marked L.

Figure 7

The next part of roof framing is shown in Figure 8 with the N and O pieces. It may be a little difficult at first to know just how to saw the N pieces, called "rafters," because the ends have to be cut slanted so that rafter N will fit tightly against ridgepole H and plate F. (See pages 40–41.)

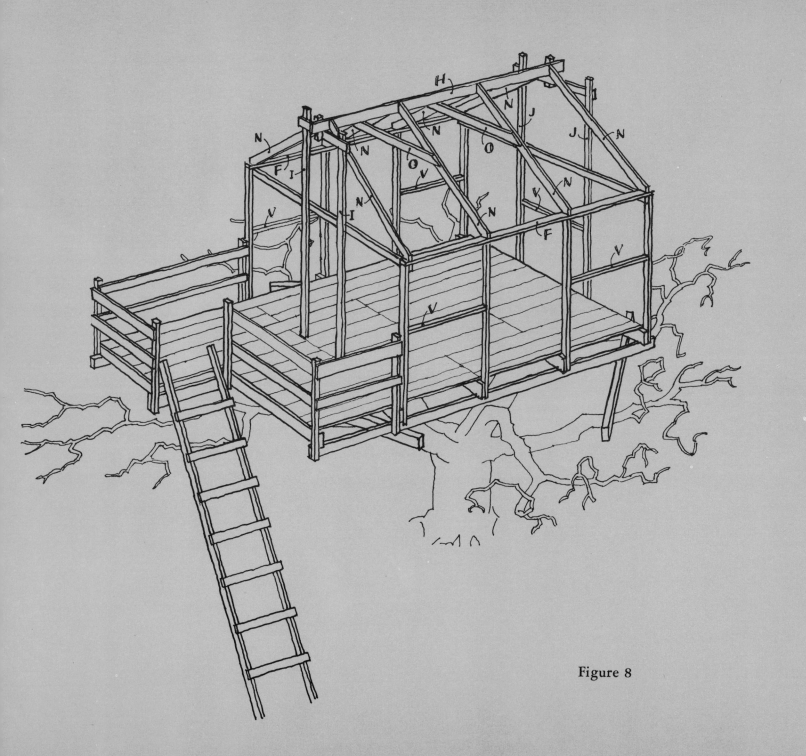

Figure 8

Here is a way to cut your 2 x 4 rafters. The detail 8a shows an H and an F piece, though drawn a little close together, as you will notice. Take a piece of 2 x 4 and fasten it on plate F as shown in 8b. Next, rest an uncut rafter N across ridgepole H and the temporary block you have placed on F, as indicated in Figure 8c. To mark the rafter cuts, place your try square on the vertical face of H, as shown in 8d, and draw a line which you will later continue across the face of the rafter. Then set the try square over the top of the temporary block and draw a horizontal cutting line. Your rafter will now look like 8e, the darkened areas being the parts to be cut away. In 8f the rafter is shown as it looks in position, fitting snugly against ridgepole H and plate F. The end of rafter N may be cut away, as shown dotted, or left projecting if you want an overhang.

Get *one rafter* cut exactly right before you start cutting the others. Use this one as a pattern to mark all the other (seven more) 2 x 4's for rafters. Then nail them up in position using sixteenpenny or twentypenny nails.

Now you can make the rafters stronger and steadier by putting up the pieces marked O (see page 39), which we call "collar ties." Put these O pieces high enough so you can walk under them, but not much higher. Nail them and saw them off at a slant even with the outside of the rafter.

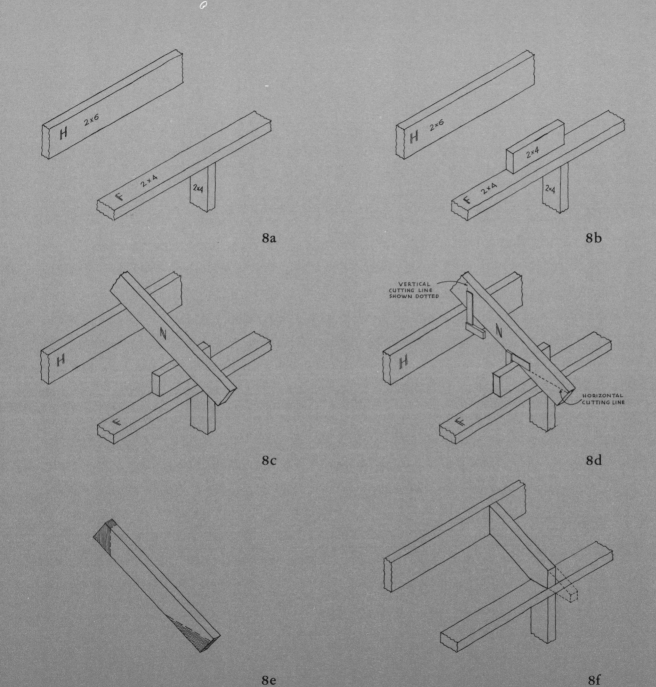

8a

8b

8c

VERTICAL
CUTTING LINE
SHOWN DOTTED

HORIZONTAL
CUTTING LINE

8d

8e

8f

SEVENTH STEP: *Framing the windows*

Before you begin to enclose your house with boards, there are a few parts of the frame that need additional reinforcement.

Cut five 2 x 4's long enough to extend horizontally between the studs in the positions shown in Figures 8 and 9. These pieces are marked V. You will also see W pieces, straight up and down. Measure the vertical space between V and the plate F and cut 2 x 4's for these pieces. This will provide a window frame at each place where a W is indicated.

Now, for a moment, turn back to Figure 7, and look at the K and L pieces which held the ridgepole in position. These pieces can be taken off because the rafters now hold the ridgepole secure. However, at this point you should reinforce the front and back rafters by adding the four pieces marked T and U in Figure 9. The T and U pieces are 2 x 4's cut like the rafters but in two sections to fit on each side of the vertical I and J pieces, front and back.

Cut pieces R and S to fit as shown in Figure 9. Nail them in place. When this is done, you will see that the end rafters and the G pieces corresponding to plates across the front and back of the house are all doubled for extra strength.

On the floor, shown again in Figure 9, you see the pieces marked P and Q. These are called "soles" and they lie between all the studs except where your door will be. These soles are 2 x 4's and will be flush on both sides with the studs; your wall boards will be nailed to them at the bottom.

Figure 9

EIGHTH STEP: *Boarding in your tree house*

Figure 9 shows you the early stages of enclosing the house with wall and roof boards.

Note that the boards in the walls run up and down. At the top they are nailed to the plates, while at the bottom they are nailed to the soles. You can nail these boards with eightpenny nails. Put the wall boarding up before you board up the roof.

The roof boards will run in the same direction as the ridgepole. If they are not long enough to reach the whole length of the roof, cut the shorter pieces as you did for the floor — that is, so that the ends will come in the middle of a rafter. Thus, as in the floor, all the ends of boards will come on a framing piece, and none will be free to bend.

Figure 10 shows you the whole house enclosed in boards.

Figure 10

45

NINTH STEP: *Finishing the house*

Finishing the house consists of putting roofing material on top of the roof boards, making and hanging a door and windows, and putting thin strips of wood (called "battens") over the cracks between boards on the walls.

Figure 11 shows a completed tree house. If you use shingles on the roof, start nailing them on at the bottom of the roof, being sure that each higher row overlaps the row below. A simpler material to use is tar paper or roofing paper which will cover your roof quite well with less expense and work.

The strips of wood over the cracks between the wall boards can be regular 1 x 2's or similar narrow strips of wood. The battens should be nailed to both boards with fourpenny or fivepenny nails. If you want a simple way to close the cracks instead of using battens, you can nail tar paper on the inside.

Door and windows at this stage are framed with the 2 x 4's of the wall frame. Either to the inside or to the outside edges of these 2 x 4's that frame the windows you can nail strips of 1 x 2 on all four sides, for what we call "stops." If your stops are flush with the outside, your window will open inward; and if they are flush with the inside, the window will open outward. Put your 1 x 2 stops at the sides and top of the door opening. Build your door, then, to go inside the 2 x 4's and up against the stops.

Figure 11

Building a Two-tree House

Building a house in two trees that are quite close together is, in some ways, easier than building a one-tree house, because the problem of making a level platform may be simpler.

It is best to have two trees no more than 10' apart. If the trunks are straight and the branches spread out fairly high above the ground, you can build your house below and clear of the branches.

SPANNING THE TREES

To begin with, take a straight board a little longer than the distance between the trees and nail one end of it at the height you want your platform. Raise the free end until it seems to be at the same height, check it by placing your spirit level on top, and then nail firmly. See Figure 12.

From 2 x 4 stock, cut four pieces of wood each 10" long. Using four 6" spikes in each block, nail one to each tree just above the board, and the other two at exactly the same height on the opposite sides of the trees. Again see Figure 12.

This done, cut two 2 x 4's long enough to go from one tree to the other with an additional foot sticking out beyond the trees at both ends. Place them on the trees so that each one rests on two of the blocks and spike them to the trees. Now you can remove the first board you put up — the one under the blocks — as shown in Figure 13.

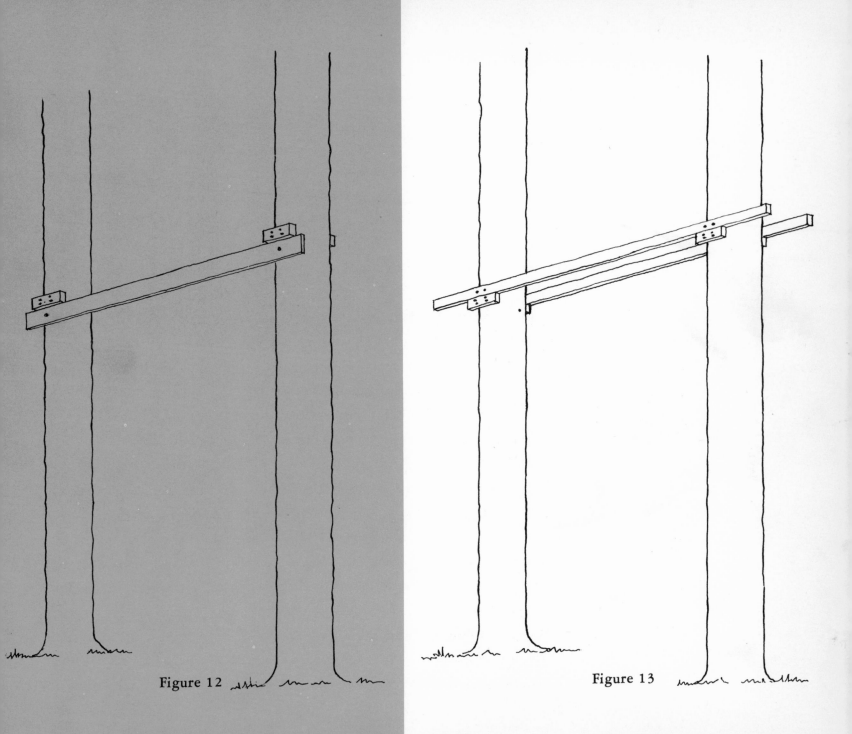

Figure 12

Figure 13

You must learn how to make a good stiff brace (the Y-shaped pieces that will support your floor timbers), because it is very useful in tree-house building. Try this out for yourself sometime. Nail the center of a board to a post so that the piece you have nailed is level with the ground. Then pull down on one side. It tips, doesn't it? Now nail it up level again, but this time put two slanted pieces under it, from the post to each end of the level board, making a Y brace. Isn't the brace much stronger than the one level board?

You will need the following pieces of wood *for each brace* (double this for two braces):

A. one 2 x 6 eight feet long

B. one 2 x 6 six feet long

C. two 2 x 4 pieces five feet six inches long

D. three 2 x 4 pieces ten inches long

E. two 2 x 2 pieces ten inches long

F. one 2 x 6 piece two feet two inches long

G. two 2 x 2 pieces twelve inches long.

It will be a good idea, as you make these pieces, to mark them with a black crayon showing the letter A or B or C, etc., as in the list above.

Take the long piece A and nail the two E pieces at the ends as shown in Figure 14. Use about four tenpenny nails in each block, being careful not to split them. (Sometimes a piece of wood will split if nails are driven too close to the edge or the end.)

Measure in from the end of the B piece, 1'7" (19 inches) and put a mark on both the narrow edges to show where you will nail the G blocks. Now nail the G blocks on with about six tenpenny nails in each block. Be sure the G block runs from your pencil mark to within 7″ of the end of B piece.

Lay the A and B pieces on a level floor. Measure and mark the middle of the A piece at the 4′ point. Find the middle of the upper end of the B piece, lay the end of B at the middle of A. The B piece should be at an exact right angle to A. Fasten them together with a D piece.

Leaving these on the floor, put the C pieces down in a Y shape, so the upper ends are under A and the lower ends are under B. With a sharp pencil draw a line very close to A and E, marking what will have to be cut off both C pieces to make them fit snugly inside A and E. Do the same at the lower ends of the C pieces, which fit at the points where B and G come together. Be careful, and try to cut off the corners so accurately that each C piece will fit perfectly at a slant between A and B and tight inside the E and G blocks. Then all four long pieces, A, B, and the two C's will lie flat on the floor and fit tightly together.

Nail F across the two C's and B as high as you can with the upper corners of F reaching the outsides of the C pieces, then trim off the lower corners at each end of F. Use two more D blocks to reinforce A and upper C on both sides.

This completes your brace. Repeat these instructions for your second brace.

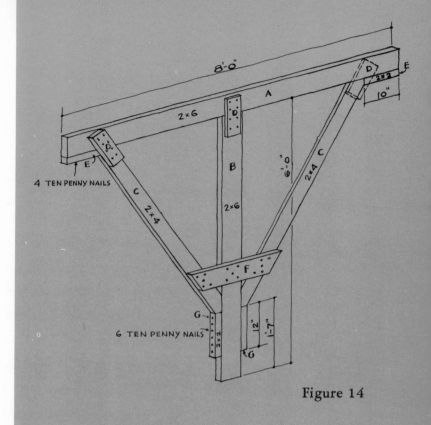

Figure 14

PUTTING UP THE BRACES AND BEAMS

You will have discovered by this time that these braces are quite heavy, and that you will need two people and perhaps a block and tackle to get them up on the trees. Lift one brace up and let it rest on the ends of the connecting poles that extend beyond each tree. Place it so that the B piece comes between the ends of the poles and flat against the tree trunk. Spike this B piece to the tree. Follow the same procedure with the second brace as shown in Figure 15.

Next we are going to put a longer piece of wood, a beam, on top of each brace. The beams are 2 x 4's marked I, each 10′ long. They lie directly on the A pieces, extending 1′ beyond A at each end. The I beams can be added to the braces either before or after the brace is nailed up in position. If the brace is not too heavy to lift with the I piece already on, it is better to attach it first, since it is easier to drive the spikes when you are working on the ground. However, if you think they will be too heavy together, put the brace up first, and then nail on the I pieces. As you will see in the next drawing, they will support the crosspieces or the joists (J) of the floor.

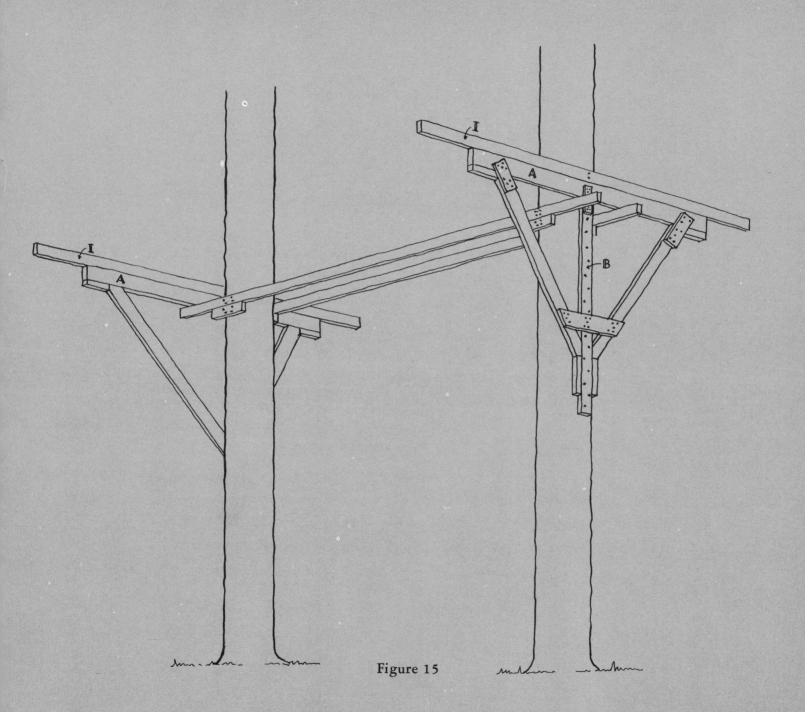

Figure 15

How you build your floor depends on the distance between the trees, and therefore the braces.

If the two braces are not more than 4'6" apart, then you can lay your floor right across on top of the I pieces, using good, sound, inch-thick boards nailed fast to both I's.

If the braces are more than 4'6" apart *but not more than 8' apart*, you should use 2" thick planks for your floor.

However if the braces are *more than 8' apart*, follow these instructions for making the floor.

See Figure 16. Cut six 2 x 6 pieces (J) exactly long enough to go between the braces, measuring from the outside edges of the I pieces. Standing them on edge on top of the I beams, put one at each side of the trees, one at each end of the I beams, and one between each pair of J's on both sides of the trees. Toenail them to the I beams.

In the drawing, you can see an extra piece of wood running crosswise between the first two J pieces on the left side. This is a piece of 2 x 6 cut to the exact length to fit between the joists here to frame a ladder hole through your floor. Nail it between the J's about 2' from the end. Boards can now be put over the joists, covering everything except the ladder hole in the corner, as in Figure 17.

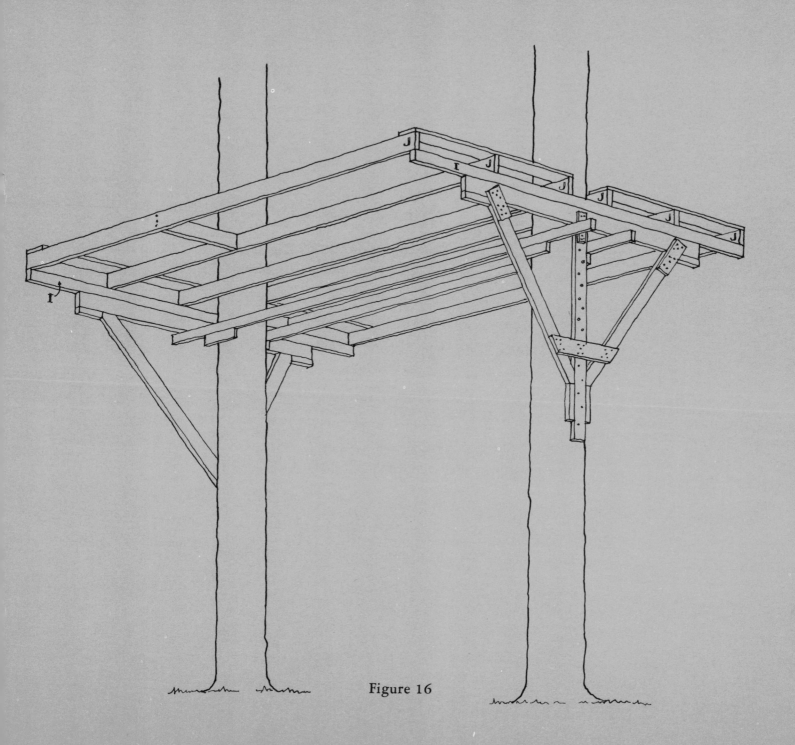

Figure 16

ENCLOSING THE PLATFORM

It is a good idea to put up a strong railing, or fence, around your floor so that there will be no chance of falling off while you build the rest. Cut about six pieces of 2 x 4's three feet long. Nail these K pieces, straight up and down, to the J's at the corners, and one in the middle of each side. They are not necessary on the ends where the trees are because you can nail the railing to the trees. Measure the distance from the corner K pieces and cut the eight L or railing pieces, again using 2 x 4 stock. Now nail your railings L all around on the K pieces and on the outside of the trees — one railing at the top of the K's and one halfway down.

By this time your building should look like Figure 17.

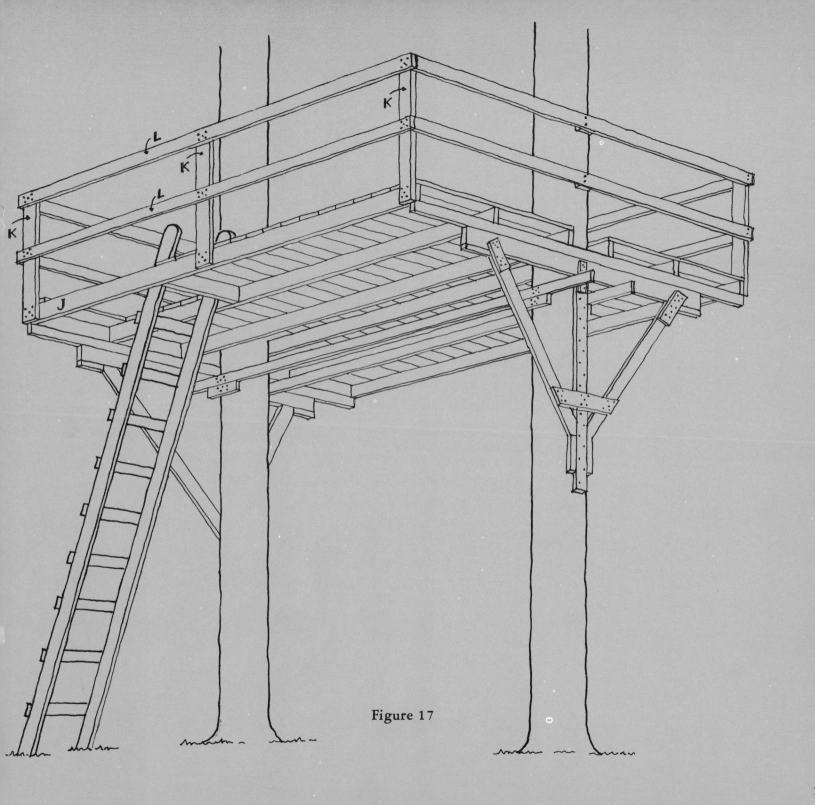

Figure 17

FRAMING WALLS AND ROOF

Now that the platform is complete, you are ready to frame the house preparatory to boarding in the walls and roof. You will find that the roof construction and wall framing for this house are different from the single tree house and that in this one it will be easier if you start with the framing of the roof.

First, nail a 2 x 4 piece (M) level between the trees and about 7′ above the floor. Then cut two 2 x 4 pieces (N) about 11′ long, or a foot longer than the I pieces on the braces. Spike these to the trees on top of the M piece, slanted so that on the side away from the ladder they are 6″ lower than in the center of the platform, as in Figure 18. This will mean that the roof on the front — or the ladder side of the house — will be about 12″ higher than at the back, and that the whole roof is one slanting flat slab, without a ridgepole as in the single tree house.

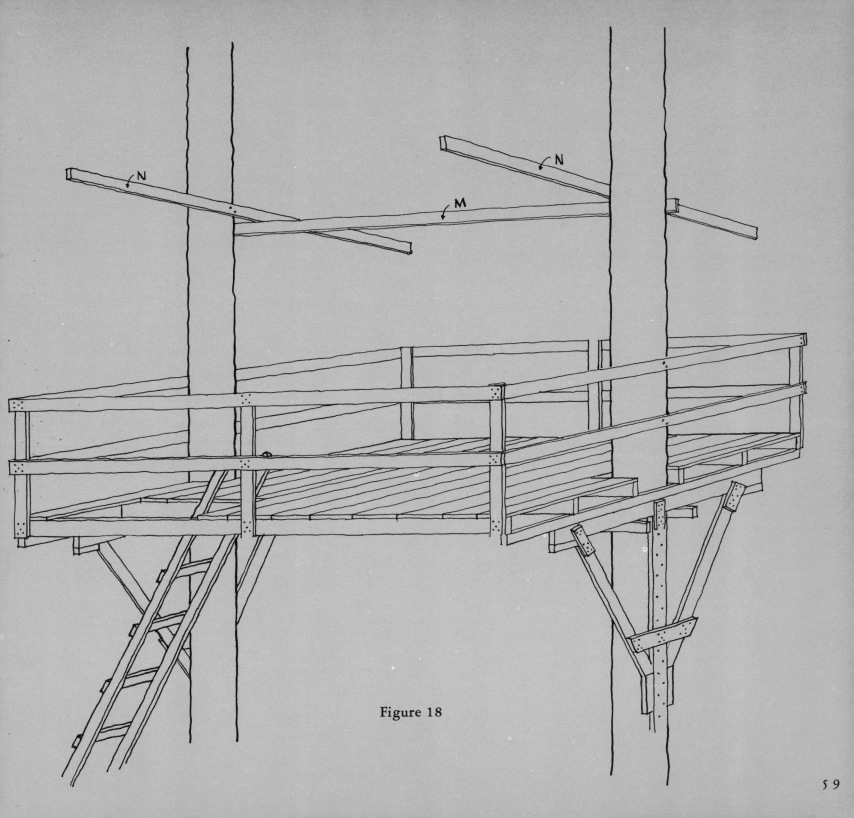

Figure 18

The two "sole" pieces marked P in Figure 19 are 2 x 4's and should be about 7½' long. Place the one nearest the ladder opening about 3" away from the opening and directly under the N piece; stand it on edge and toenail it into the platform. The sole piece on the other side must be the same distance in from the front edge of the platform. At the ends of the sole pieces P and extending up to the N pieces, nail the two Q pieces and the two R pieces straight up and down. These are also 2 x 4's. Check these with your plumb line to be sure that they are vertical.

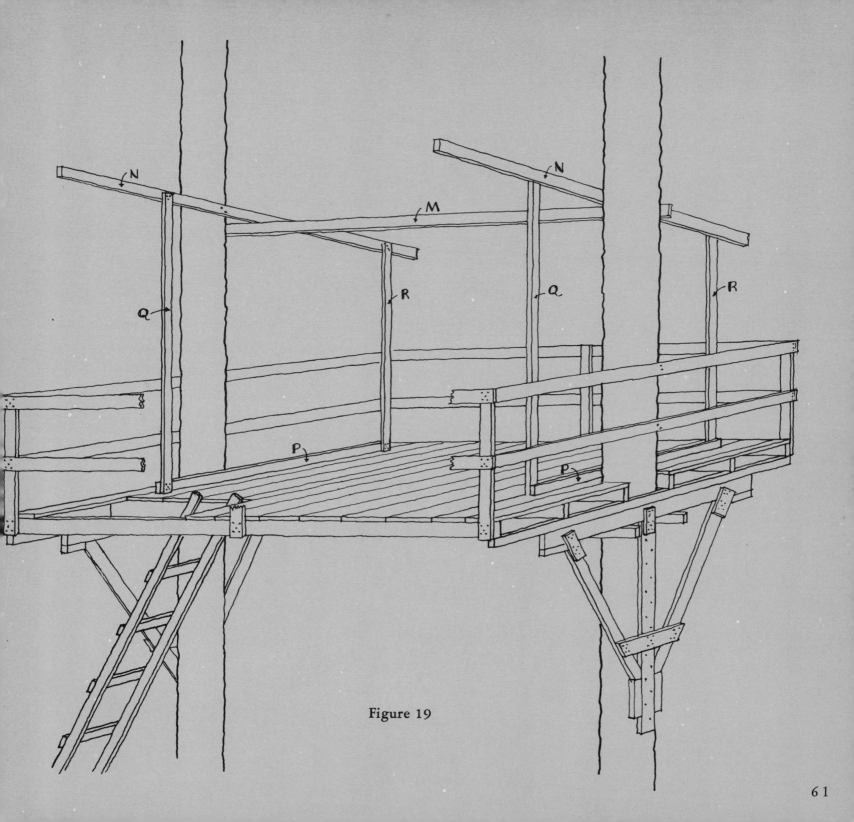

Figure 19

In Figure 20 you will see three more 2 x 4's added to the framing of the house: a third sole piece (U) running across the back of the house, and the two plate pieces front and back, S and T, which will later support the roof framing. When you put these up, check with your spirit level to be sure that they are level.

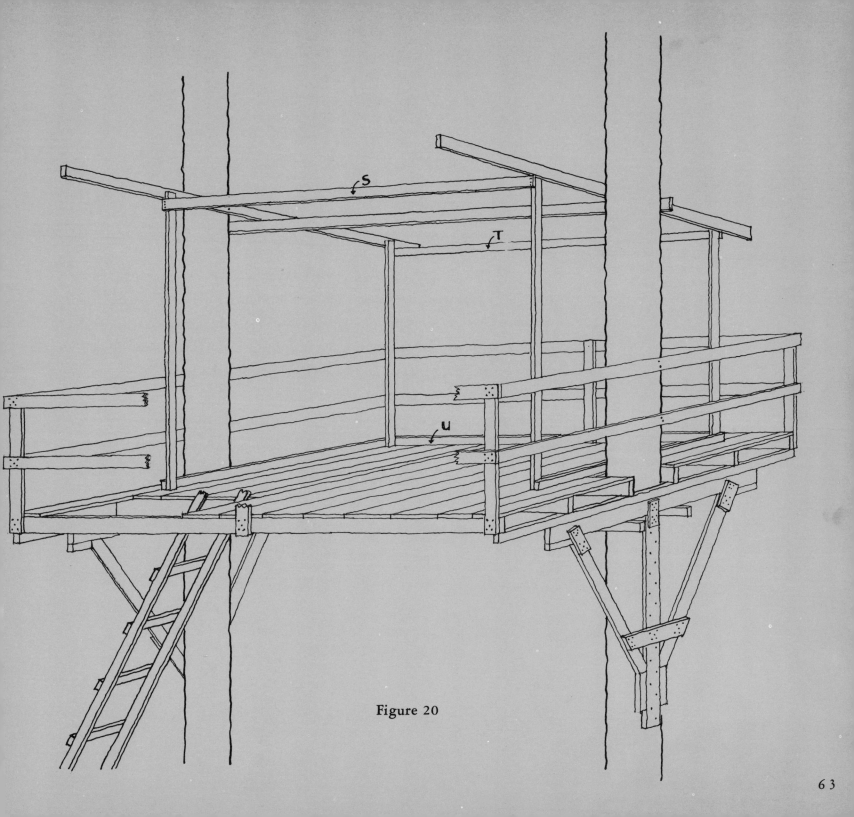

Figure 20

The fourth sole piece in front, marked V in Figure 21, is in two sections, allowing a 2′ opening for the door. The two uprights (W) on either side of the door space are the door frame. They are 2 x 4's and should be nailed into both the sole and the plate. If you want a window in front, you will have to add two more upright pieces (X) and the two level Y pieces in between for the window frame. To complete the framing of the house you will need two or three more rafters, N pieces, the same length as the first two and evenly spaced between them; toenail them to the plates front and back and to the M piece in the middle.

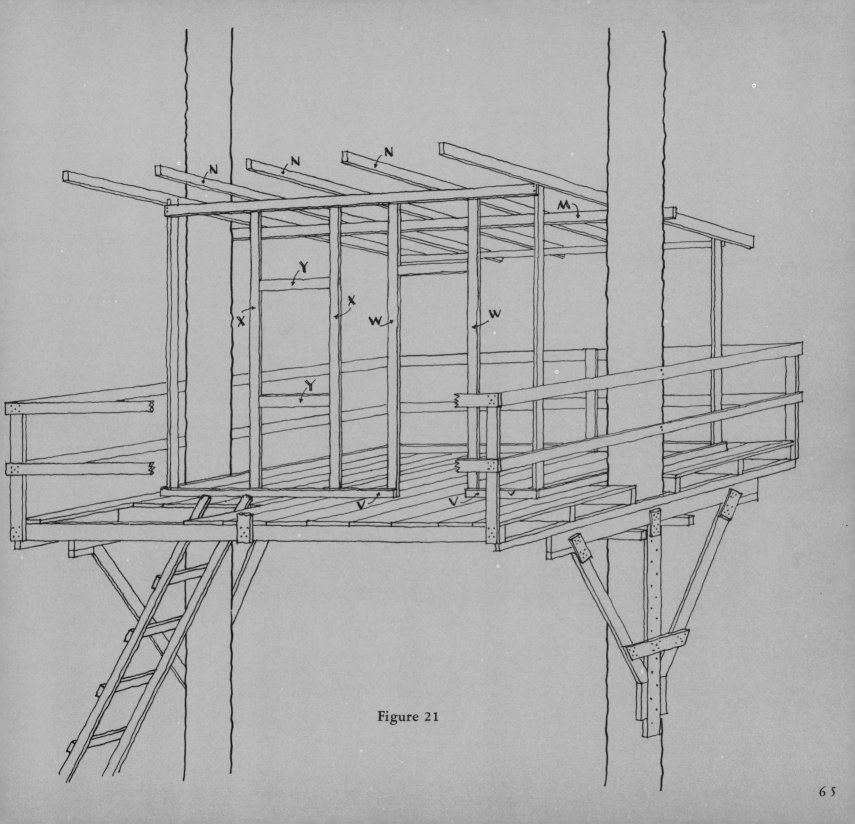

Figure 21

Once you have finished the frame, you are ready to enclose the building. First nail the roof boards across the rafters. In Figure 22, you will see the wall boards nailed up both horizontally and vertically. Begin nailing them horizontally; if you want a more finished and weatherproof house, add a second layer of boards running vertically. In the front, since you have a 2′ wide porch, you will find it easy to attach the wall boards to the outside of the frame. However, on the other three sides it is simpler to work from the inside of the house. If you do, the framing of the back and sides will be exposed but the walls themselves will be just as satisfactory.

Although I have given the steps for one-tree and two-tree houses you will find that the many variations in tree shapes require slight changes from my rules. These you can make with a little ingenuity, but remember to build strongly. Avoid the use of too small nails. For framing, I have advised tenpenny nails and spikes; for flooring and boarding the roof and side walls, eightpenny nails are large enough.

And work safely. Never forget that you are on a ladder or a platform. Place the ladder so that it is firmly held at top and bottom.

Finally, you will have your own ideas for special touches and decorative effects, perhaps painting the house and platform, as Bob and Ricky did when they built a tree house and developed it until it reached the ground and became a two-story cottage instead.

You probably won't go that far, but with some imagination you can make your tree house much more exciting than the basic houses I have described here.

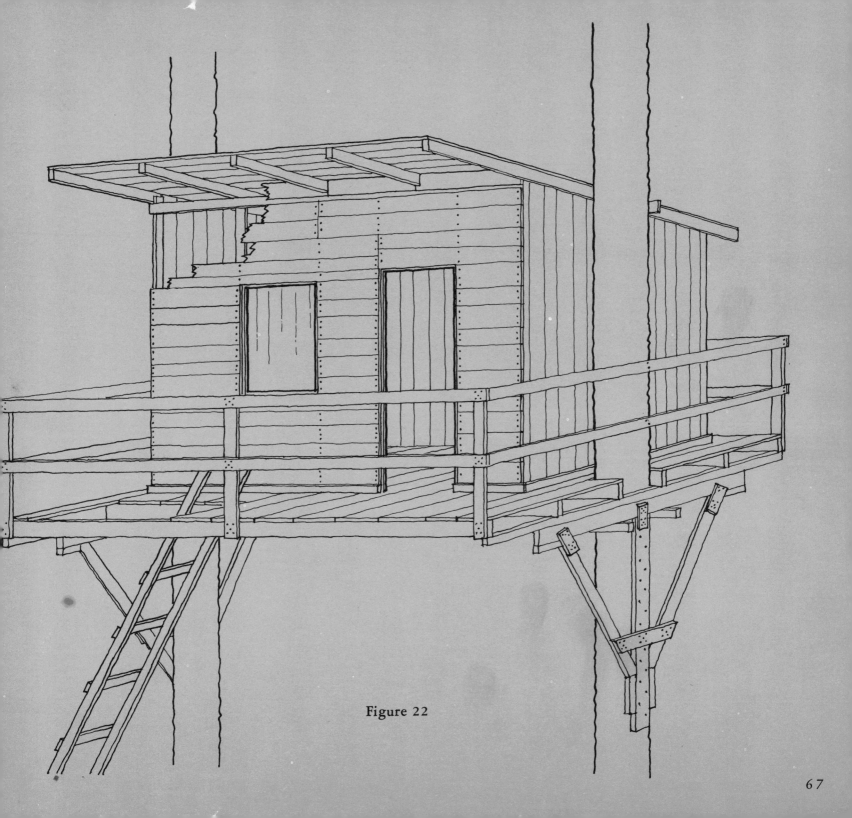

Figure 22